BRINGING BACK THE ANIMALS

Never before has so much of the rich life of our planet been under threat as now. The threat comes from the activity of human beings all over the earth, from the pollution of our air and seas, to the destruction of the rainforests. When the home of any one of the world's animals is destroyed or polluted, that animal could end up dying out for ever.

In the last fifty years, over half of the world's rain forest has been destroyed, and with it the homes of vast numbers of rare animals and plants. So what took 100,000,000 years to evolve could be destroyed in less than 100 years.

The graceful and intelligent Blue Whale, the largest mammal on earth, is one of the animals we have nearly hunted to extinction. The beautiful Blue Macaw is dying out because its rainforest home is being destroyed. If we are going to stop the destruction, we must change the way we treat the earth. Friends of the Earth are trying to get people to protect our planet, and the homes of all its animals.

If you want to help us in our fight, you can find out more about us at the address at the end of the book. If you are interested in any one animal, there may be a special organisation that is trying to protect it. A short list of some of the main ones is included at the back of this book.

D1287593

TEXT COPYRIGHT © 1991 TERESA KENNEDY
ILLUSTRATIONS COPYRIGHT © SUE WILLIAMS

ALL RIGHTS RESERVED, INCLUDING THE RIGHT TO REPRODUCE THIS BOOK OR PORTIONS THEREOF IN ANY FORM.
PUBLISHED IN THE UNITED STATES BY AMETHYST BOOKS, P.O. BOOK 895, WOODSTOCK, N.Y. 12498
AND IN THE UNITED KINGDOM BY AMETHYST BOOKS, LIME TREE HOUSE, SWALCLIFFE, BANBURY,
OXON OX15 5EH.

ISBN 0-944256-06-6

AMETHYST CHILDREN'S BOOKS ARE DISTRIBUTED IN THE UNITED STATES BY THE TALMAN CO., NEW YORK
AND IN THE UNITED KINGDOM BY RAGGED BEARS, HANTS

Bringing Back The Animals

Written by

Teresa Kennedy

Illustrations by

Sue Williams

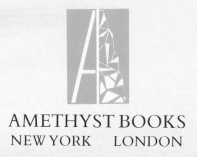

AMETHYST BOOKS

NEW YORK   LONDON

The Giant Panda

~

Once in the highlands of western China, thousands of Giant Pandas roamed. A panda is a kind of bear. When a baby panda is born, it weighs just a few ounces, yet when they are grown, they can weigh as much as three hundred pounds (150 Kg)! As big as they are, the Giant Panda is a gentle, friendly-looking creature with a large head and a beautiful black-and-white fur coat.

Pandas eat the leaves, shoots and stems of the bamboo plant, which grows wild in a kind of forest. A creature that weighs so much needs a lot to eat, though, and the pandas don't always have enough. As farmers clear the forest land to plant their crops, much of the bamboo is destroyed, and so it is harder and harder for the pandas to find the food they need.

Now, there are only 800 Giant Pandas left. But caring people have seen the panda's problem and are trying to help. The Chinese government has set aside land for the pandas to live on, and paths have been cleared between bamboo forests, to make it easier for the pandas to get from place to place. That way, the pandas can not only find enough food - they can find each other, mate and bring more pandas into the world.

The Grevy's Zebra

~

These zebras are named after the scientist who first identified them. Grevy's Zebras, like all zebras, live in Africa where they have wandered over open plains – called savannah – for centuries.

This type of zebra is the least like a horse and more like a donkey than any other zebra. It has narrow, close-set stripes, a slightly rounder head and ears, and a voice that is very much like a donkey's. These zebras are probably the oldest variety of zebra on earth.

Grevy's Zebras live in family groups, and wander over huge territories. Except for the fact that they can run very fast and over great distances, the zebra has very few natural defences against predators. They are susceptible to all sorts of attacks from other animals as well as those from hunters.

People have become extremely concerned about all varieties of zebras, and rightly so. Many varieties of zebra have already become completely extinct due to irresponsible big-game hunters, intrusion into their natural habitats and scattering of the huge family groups they need and depend on to survive. Recognising the problem at last, several African governments have now banded together to outlaw the hunting of zebra and to establish wild game preserves where these zebra can roam and live without any threat to their herds. While still in danger in the wild, Grevy's Zebra seems to be thriving in these well-protected environments.

The Bottle-Nosed Dolphin

The Bottle-nosed Dolphin is named for its long, well-defined beak. These dolphins dwell in the waters of the North Atlantic and the Mediterranean oceans. Marked by their long beaks and rounded heads, dolphins have greyish, fish-like bodies, and are among the best and fastest swimmers of the ocean, easily able to keep pace with many ships and boats.

The dolphin has a brain that is very close in size, shape and configuration to the human brain. Dolphins have been found to have a language, a highly developed society, the ability to learn complex skills and emotional bonds to mates and young that are very similar to the way human beings feel about each other.

In recent years, scientists have begun to study the dolphin in earnest, convinced that there is a genuine possibility of breaking the language barrier and learning to actually communicate with another species for the first time in the history of the world.

Given what we know about the dolphin, it is hard to believe that these wonderful creatures may well find themselves on the endangered list. The reason for this is that certain kinds of commercial fishing nets, particularly those used for tuna, also catch and needlessly kill dolphins.

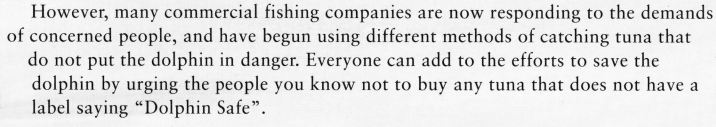

However, many commercial fishing companies are now responding to the demands of concerned people, and have begun using different methods of catching tuna that do not put the dolphin in danger. Everyone can add to the efforts to save the dolphin by urging the people you know not to buy any tuna that does not have a label saying "Dolphin Safe".

The Jaguar

The Jaguar is the king of the rainforest. These magnificent cats live in the jungles and forests deep in South America. They resemble their cousins the leopards with rounded heads and beautiful spotted coats, but they are larger and heavier, with a shorter tail.

Like all wild cats, the jaguar requires wilderness to roam and hunt. One jaguar's territory can range from three miles (5km) in diameter to as much as fifteen miles (25km) in diameter. Because they are such heavy animals, jaguars are not good climbers and hunt mostly on the ground. For this reason, they need a hunting territory that includes high grass, trees or rocks for cover, so they may better stalk their prey. Jaguars swim well and are capable of extraordinary feats of strength. One account records a jaguar tugging a full grown horse for a distance of nearly ninety yards (80m) to the edge of a river, then swimming across the river with the horse in tow!

The jaguar is in danger because his natural habitat, the rainforest, is being burned away to clear the land for farms. As the area of rainforest shrinks, the jaguar has less and less of the territory he needs to survive.

Many people feel that the destruction of the rainforest is bad for not only the jaguar, but for the whole earth. All over the world, concerned people are working to save the rainforest from destruction, and making others aware of the problem. As people work to save these forests, they are also working to save the jaguar and to preserve the kingdom where he rules.

The African Elephant

~

Huge herds of elephants once thundered across the African plains. A hundred years ago, there were three million elephants living there. Now, there are less than half a million left.

Though the whale is the largest animal in the sea, the African elephant is the largest animal living on land. Fully grown, these magnificent creatures can weigh as much as six and a half tons, and stand ten to thirteen feet (3-4m) high! Their beautiful ivory tusks, which grow out from either side of the trunk, can be longer than a human being is tall.

But it is because of their tusks that the African elephant is in danger. For too long, people valued jewelry and other items made of ivory, unaware that so many of these elephants were being hunted and killed for their tusks. Even though an African elephant can live for decades, they do not reproduce quickly. So when a whole family of elephants is hunted down, it takes many years to re-establish a herd.

Now, African governments have joined together to pass tough new laws against elephant hunting. But illegal hunting, or poaching, still goes on. The reason for this is because Africa is a very poor country, and the tusks can sometimes be sold for far more money than an African farmer would make in a whole year.

The solution to the problem is clear. The only way to help the African elephant survive is to stop poaching. And the only way to stop poaching is for everyone to stop buying items made of ivory. If no one buys ivory, elephant hunting will stop because the poachers will be unable to make any money selling tusks.

The Bald Eagle

~

The Bald Eagle is found at home all over North America and Mexico. They migrate for huge distances, and may easily be found spending the winter in Florida, and the summer in Canada.

They are among the largest of the eagle family, usually over two and a half feet (0.8m) in length with a wing span of up to seven and a half feet (2.3m). The females of this group are generally larger and heavier than the males, which is a bit unusual in the world of birds. Their reputation for being "bald" comes from the fact that their head feathers are usually white, in contrast to the dark and golden brown plumage of their wings and back.

With their strong beaks and large talons, these birds are able to snatch fish from the water and smaller birds in flight.

The bald eagle is the national symbol for the United States, and the fact that this revered symbol became endangered served to alert Americans to the terrible problems of pesticides in the environment. Both adult eagles and eggs began to show traces of toxic chemicals and as the eagle population began to diminish, concern over environmental issues began to rise.

Now, environmentalists and scientists all over the country are monitoring the bald eagles, and efforts to hatch and protect young eagles in various parts of the country have met with increased success. Though there is still reason for concern, the numbers of bald eagles are on the rise and, with continued care, their survival is assured. More importantly, the plight of the bald eagle has served to make for stronger laws and regulations regarding the use of chemicals, and that will help make for a better, healthier future for all living things.

The Polar Bear

~

The Polar Bear takes his name from his natural home - the North Pole. Polar bears could be said to live at the very top of the world, in the coastal waters and ice floes of the Arctic Ocean.

The polar bear is the largest and heaviest of all bears. An adult polar bear stands four feet high (1.2m) at the shoulder, and standing on his hind legs is almost twice as tall. Though they live in one of the coldest places on earth, polar bears are perfectly suited to the ice and snow because they are protected by a thick white fur coat that not only keeps them warm, but helps them to blend into their surroundings.

Some scientists even claim that when a polar bear goes to hunt for food, he covers his black nose with one paw, to help him blend more completely into the snowy background, and remain unseen by his prey.

For years, the polar bear was hunted by Eskimos for its fur, and by big-game hunters. World governments have passed new laws to protect the polar bear from hunters, but people still have reason to be concerned.

The polar bear needs the natural cold of the Arctic to survive. Many scientists believe the earth's atmosphere is gradually warming up and causing what has been called "the greenhouse effect". This means simply that too much pollution in the atmosphere will cause temperatures to rise. If temperatures rise too much, the ice floes in the Arctic will begin to melt and the polar bear will have nowhere to live.

Everyone helps the polar bear when they take the time and care to help their environment. If we work together to reduce pollution by recycling and conservation, we can help preserve the icy kingdom ruled by the "Lord of the Arctic"- the great white bear who lives on top of the world.

The Water Buffalo

~

The lakes and rivers of Southeast Asia are home to a beast known as the Water Buffalo. Massive and slow-moving, the water buffalo stands as tall as a man at the shoulder, yet can weigh over two thousand pounds (1000kg)! The water buffalo's head is crowned by two huge, crescent-shaped horns.

As you might suspect from its name, this buffalo needs water to survive—not just for drinking, but to stay cool during the day. At sunrise during warm weather, water buffalo will go to the nearest riverbank, wade into the water and mud and simply stay there until the sun goes down. Those huge horns also serve as a shovel. Oftentimes during the day the buffalo will dip his horns deep into the mud of the riverbank, scoop some up, and throw it on his back to serve as a kind of blanket to keep him cool.

Though there were once huge herds of these buffalo roaming the plains of Southeast Asia, they have become extremely rare and now live only on special reserves. Because they are so huge and slow-moving, these buffalo were easy prey for hunters, who used their meat and also sought their crescent-shaped horns to make into various objects.

Sadly, the water buffalo is also terribly susceptible to certain kinds of cattle disease. Due to the fact that a wild creature cannot be treated for these diseases the way a farm animal can, thousands have died out.

That is why the remaining water buffalo have been rounded up and allowed to live in special reserve to protect them. Though there are hardly any of these creatures left in the wild, reserves like these will protect the buffalo and allow them to build up their numbers until hopefully there are once again enough water buffalo to roam the plains and lounge on the muddy riverbanks of Southeast Asia.

The Tiger

~

The Tiger is the largest living cat on earth. They are beautiful creatures with striped fur coats who live in Asia and India. A full-grown tiger measures six feet (1.8 m) over his head and body, and his tail can be another three feet (0.9 m) long. Most weigh more than a dozen children put together!

As big as he is, the tiger has a huge appetite. They are meat-eaters and need almost twenty pounds (10 kg) of meat a day to stay healthy. Tigers eat deer, elk, lynx, hare, fish and domestic animals. Because he needs so much food to survive, the tiger needs a lot of space in which to hunt. Tiger territories can be as large as ten square miles (25 sq km). Powerful and muscular, the tiger is well-equipped for his hunting tasks. Yet they are also extremely graceful creatures. Tigers can leap great distances and are able to jump down onto their prey from trees or rocks above.

Like many other animals, the tiger was hunted for its fur and because of its reputation as a dangerous man-eater. Sadly, their numbers began to shrink. Since tigers do not live in groups, they cannot protect each other from hunters, and they also do not breed very often. Tigers will mate and have cubs only every four or five years, so when the tiger population shrinks, it can take a very long time to build it back up again.

Now, particularly in India, the government has stepped in to protect and save the tiger from extinction, by making new laws and by setting up special reserves where tigers can meet, mate and build the tiger population up once again. Though these measures take time, they do help. If more people in more countries get involved, we can save the largest cat on earth.

The Blue Whale

Blue Whales have lived in the ocean for 50 million years. These whales are bigger than any other animal in the world. Try to imagine a creature longer than 30 cars parked end to end, or one that weighs more than two thousand people! That is how big a blue whale can be.

Whales like to travel and explore. One whale can travel all of the oceans in the world in less than a year. They sing to each other under water so they won't get lost or lonely. Even though whales are big, they are peaceful, intelligent animals. And it is sad that there are hardly any Blue Whales left.

For too many years, people have hunted these whales – for their meat, bones, oil and blubber. Now there is no reason to hunt whales anymore because there are lots of other, better ways to make these things.

In 1948, concerned people from all different countries started The International Whaling Commission, which tries to stop people from hunting not only Blue Whales, but many other kinds of whales as well. But people do not always obey the laws, and some illegal hunting continues. Today many other groups have joined in to help and protect these whales by tracking them, learning about them, and rescuing them when they are in trouble. Most important of all, they teach people about whales and how precious their lives have become.

The Hooded Cobra

~

Deep in Asia lives the Hooded Cobra. These snakes take their name from the fact that when they raise their heads to strike an enemy, they spread their ribs, forming an arc-shaped hood. These cobras vary a great deal in appearance, and can be light brown, brown, olive green or black with stripes. The underside of the cobra's throat is almost always a creamy yellow or white. They can grow to lengths of up to seven feet (2.22m) long.

Though the cobra prefers a wet, warm environment, these snakes are very adaptable and can appear almost anywhere – the jungle, in rice fields or farmland, or even in a city park or back yard! They eat mice, lizards, rats, birds, frogs and toads.

But though the cobra is able to adapt to many different environments, human beings have a much harder time adapting to the cobra. These snakes have a deadly bite, and are responsible for many, many deaths every year. For years, cobras have been hated and feared in that part of the world, and were killed for their skins, for their danger to human beings, and sometimes for no reason at all. As a result, many species of cobra are now on the endangered list.

Still, people are learning more about the cobra all the time. They are beginning to realize the cobra's bite is its only way of defending itself against enemies and intruders, and that they will not strike unless threatened or disturbed. Scientists have discovered that, in tiny amounts, certain kinds of cobra venom can be used as a medicine to help those who have been bitten by other snakes. Farmers are also learning to make friends with the cobra. They have discovered that, if left in peace, the cobra can help keep their crops free of other troublesome pests, like mice, rats and lizards.

The European Lynx

~

The Lynx is an unusual-looking wildcat with large pointed ears, long limbs, and a kind of beard around its face. Once, the lynx lived all over Europe, roaming mostly through the mountains and forests.

This cat has a fine fur coat that can range from a yellowish grey to red. They can have spots or not, depending on where they are found. Northern lynxes tend to have more prominently spotted coats than do their Southern cousins. The lynx's large, pointed ears have long tufts of hair growing out of them, and scientists think that in some way these tufts help give the lynx a keener sense of hearing than most other creatures. Their paws are also very large and thickly padded with fur, to help to keep the swift-footed lynx from sinking in the snow.

Like most wild cats, lynxes are great hunters and need a huge territory to roam in order to seek out their prey. If the supply of small animals and food is good and easy to find, this territory can be as small as forty or so acres. But if food is scarce, a single lynx can roam an area of as much as four thousand acres.

In the past, the lynx was hunted for fur and because of the danger people thought this cat presented to farm animals. But though they were once killed in large numbers, people recognized the problem in time. Now, the European lynx is protected in almost all countries. People have discovered that if left alone in the wild, the lynx is not truly dangerous to other animals, but can actually help farmers by feeding only on weak or sick creatures that would probably not have survived anyway.

The European lynx is one of the great success stories in bringing back the animals. The number of lynx is increasing all the time, and thanks to caring people, good laws and governments, their survival is almost assured.

Friends of the Earth

Friends of the Earth is an organisation that works to improve the environment. We do this by trying to talk to governments, the people who run factories and industry, and anybody else who can help. We try to persuade them to protect the environment. We also let people know what is the environment by producing leaflets and books such as this one.

Friends of the Earth campaign in many areas. These include the destruction of the world's tropical rainforest, water pollution, waste and recycling, the use of energy, countryside, agriculture and transport. Friends of the Earth produce a variety of materials for children. To get a full list and to find out more about our work why not write to us at :

Friends of the Earth, 26 - 28 Underwood Street, London N1 7JQ.

Friends of the Earth also has a special family membership so why not encourage your parents to join ?

SCHOOL FRIENDS

School Friends is a special service which is available to schools from Friends of the Earth. Through School Friends, schools can receive up to date information and contribute to the vital work of Friends of the Earth. Schools receive a special starter pack on joining, then a pack of teaching material every September. Why not get your school or teacher to join School Friends and protect the homes of wildlife throughout the planet?